NATURE'S REVENGE

BLUSTERY BLIZZARDS

CHARLOTTE TAYLOR

Gareth Stevens PUBLISHING

Please visit our website, www.garethstevens.com. For a free color catalog of all our high-quality books, call toll free 1-800-542-2595 or fax 1-877-542-2596.

Library of Congress Cataloging-in-Publication Data
Names: Taylor, Charlotte, 1978- author.
Title: Blustery blizzards / Charlotte Taylor.
Description: New York : Gareth Stevens Publishing, [2023] | Series: Nature's revenge | Includes index.
Identifiers: LCCN 2021051375 (print) | LCCN 2021051376 (ebook) | ISBN 9781538280447 (set) | ISBN 9781538280454 (library binding) | ISBN 9781538280430 (paperback) | ISBN 9781538280461 (ebook)
Subjects: LCSH: Blizzards–Juvenile literature.
Classification: LCC QC926.37 .T38 2023 (print) | LCC QC926.37 (ebook) | DDC 551.55/5–dc23/eng/20211122
LC record available at https://lccn.loc.gov/2021051375
LC ebook record available at https://lccn.loc.gov/2021051376

Portions of this work were originally authored by Jill Keppeler and published as *Blasted by Blizzards*. All new material in this edition was authored by Charlotte Taylor.

Published in 2023 by
Gareth Stevens Publishing
29 East 21st Street
New York, NY 10010

Designer: Leslie Taylor
Editor: Megan Quick

Photo credits: Cover (blizzard photo) justoomm/Shutterstock.com; pp. 1–32 (icons-series artwork) Vector by/Shutterstock.com; pp. 1–32 (hazard tape-series artwork) DDevecee/Shutterstock.com; p. 5 CreativeAngela/Shutterstock.com; p. 7 Triff/Shutterstock.com; p. 9 Andrei Stepanov/Shutterstock.com; p. 11 (main) buradaki/Shutterstock.com; p. 11 https://www.nasa.gov/feature/goddard/2017/scientists-receive-preliminary-data-from-goes-16s-magnetometer; p. 13 Alex Kosev/Shutterstock.com; p. 15 Chiyacat/Shutterstock.com; p. 17 (map art) PSboom/Shutterstock.com; p. 19 (top) The Protected Art Archive/Alamy Stock Photo; p. 19 (bottom) https://commons.wikimedia.org/wiki/File:Brooklyn_Museum_-_Blizzard_of_March_1888,_Brooklyn_-_Breading_G._Way_-_overall.jpg; p. 20 (plow) Perutskyi Petro/Shutterstock.com; p. 21 LINDSAY DEDARIO/REUTERS/Alamy Stock Photo; p. 23 BlueRingMedia/Shutterstock.com; p. 25 https://commons.wikimedia.org/wiki/File:Early_January_2018_Nor%27easter_2018-01-04_1345Z.jpg; p. 27 Ink Drop/Shutterstock.com; p. 29 Luka Hercigonja/Shutterstock.com.

Printed in the United States of America

Some of the images in this book illustrate individuals who are models. The depictions do not imply actual situations or events.

CPSIA compliance information: Batch #CS23GS: For further information contact Gareth Stevens, New York, New York at 1-800-542-2595.

CONTENTS

Words in the glossary appear in **bold** type the first time they are used in the text.

SERIOUS SNOW

Snow day! Big flakes fall softly and cover the ground in a white blanket. Kids go sledding and make snowballs. Snow can be pretty and fun. But some snowstorms are different. They bring high winds and blowing snow. They can be very dangerous. These storms are called blizzards. Over the years, blizzards have become more common. Many scientists say this is because of **climate change**.

Weather is different depending on where you live. Some places get very hot. Other places may have lots of rain. An area's weather over a long period of time is called its climate. Earth's climate is changing, and this is causing lots of problems for our planet. One of these problems is **extreme** weather. And blizzards are definitely extreme!

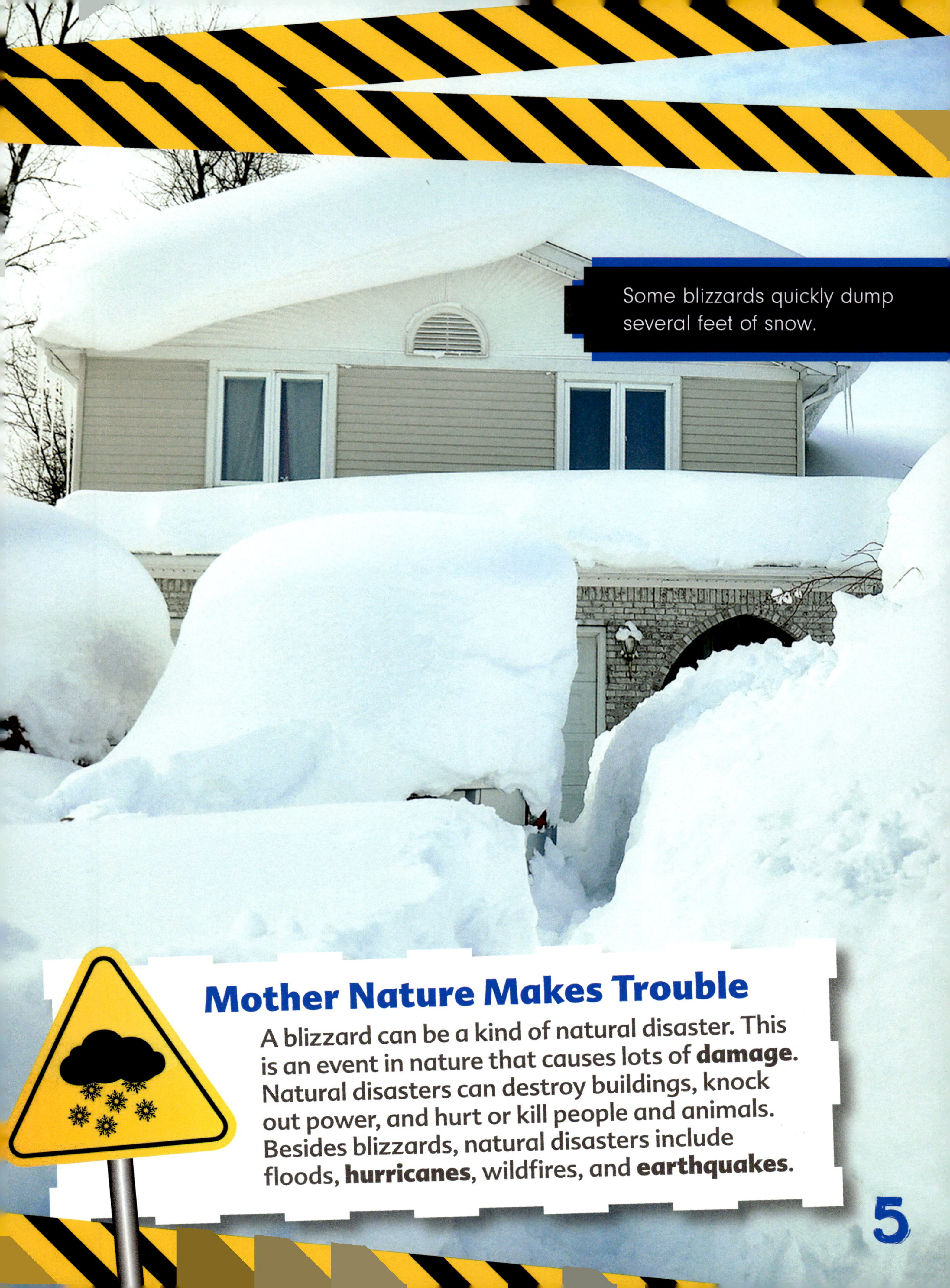

Some blizzards quickly dump several feet of snow.

Mother Nature Makes Trouble

A blizzard can be a kind of natural disaster. This is an event in nature that causes lots of **damage**. Natural disasters can destroy buildings, knock out power, and hurt or kill people and animals. Besides blizzards, natural disasters include floods, **hurricanes**, wildfires, and **earthquakes**.

SNOW SCIENCE

Most blizzards have at least some snowfall, though not all do. This means that it needs to be cold outside. Water freezes at 32°F (0°C), so the air in the **atmosphere** must be at least that cold for snow to fall. It will not snow if the temperature near ground level is higher than about 41°F (5°C).

In addition to cold temperatures, there also needs to be water in the air in order for it to snow. The water freezes and forms tiny ice crystals. These ice crystals stick together to make snowflakes.

The Water Cycle

Water in oceans, lakes, and rivers **evaporates** as it is warmed by the sun. It rises into the air as water **vapor**. As it gets higher in the atmosphere, it cools and becomes a liquid again. This is called condensation. The water gathers in clouds and falls back to Earth as rain or snow.

A close-up photo of snowflakes shows the beautiful designs made by the ice crystals.

SNOWSTORM VS. BLIZZARD

Snowfall may be light or heavy. But even huge snowstorms are not always blizzards. In order to be a blizzard, a storm must have strong winds and snow that is falling or blowing. These conditions must last for at least three hours, and winds must blow at least 35 miles (56.3 km) per hour.

A blizzard must also make it very difficult to see. This is called low visibility. If you went out in a blizzard, you would not be able to see more than one-quarter mile (0.4 km) in front of you. It would be very easy to get lost. This is just one reason blizzards are so dangerous.

From the Ground Up

Some blizzards produce little or no actual snowfall. Instead, snow that is already on the ground is picked up by heavy winds and blown around. This is known as a ground blizzard. These dangerous storms often come with very low temperatures and wind **gusts** of 50 to 60 miles (80.5 to 96.6 km) per hour.

A whiteout happens when blowing snow makes it almost impossible to see anything around you.

TROUBLE ON THE WAY

The wind, cold, and snow that come with blizzards can cause lots of trouble. It's important to know a storm is coming so you can be prepared. Meteorologists are scientists who study weather, climate, and the atmosphere. They can warn you if a blizzard is coming.

Meteorologists have many tools that help them understand weather. They use computers to study weather patterns from the past and **predict** what might be coming. **Radar** tells scientists about winds, clouds, and water in the air. But even with these tools, predicting snow is tricky. A few degrees warmer or colder can mean the difference between rain and snow. Some scientists say snow is the hardest kind of weather to predict.

The GOES-16 is a weather satellite that was sent into space in 2016. It collects information about the weather and sends it back to Earth.

Storm Warnings

The National Weather Service (NWS) lets us know when severe weather is on its way. One to three days ahead of time, the NWS will issue a blizzard watch. This means there is a 50 to 80 percent chance of a blizzard. If it continues, a blizzard warning comes next. There is now a very high chance that the storm will hit in 12 to 36 hours.

BE SMART

If a meteorologist says a blizzard is on the way, get ready! Make sure you have plenty of supplies. A basic emergency kit should include bottled water, food, medicines, a **battery**-powered radio, flashlights, and extra batteries. You will also need snow shovels and extra clothes and blankets. Be sure to have a fully charged cell phone.

Once the blizzard arrives, do not go outside. Being out in freezing conditions could cause hypothermia and frostbite. Hypothermia is when a person's body temperature gets dangerously low. Signs include shivering, numbness, confusion, and sleepiness. Frostbite is when the skin freezes. Signs of frostbite include loss of feeling in the skin or a change in the skin's color.

An emergency kit should include many of these important items, like ready-to-eat foods in case you do not have power for cooking.

Stuck in the Snow

If you get stuck on the road in a storm, do not leave the car! Keep an emergency kit in the trunk with the same supplies as the one in your house. Turn on the motor for 10 minutes an hour for warmth, keeping the window open a bit for fresh air. Tie a bright cloth outside so others can see you.

CLEANING UP

The winds have died down, and the snow has stopped blowing. The storm is over! But often, the problems have just begun. There's usually a lot to clean up after a blizzard. There may be a lot of snow to clear. Buildings may be in bad shape, and power lines may be down. People may be trapped in their homes, businesses, or schools.

Cars might be stuck on roads that need to be cleared. Cities where people are used to dealing with snow may be able to send out many snowplows to clean up. If a city isn't used to snow, this might be an even bigger problem!

The cleanup after a blizzard may last a lot longer than the storm itself.

The Weight of Snow

Not all blizzards bring loads of snow, but many do. Major snowfall can create lots of problems. One reason is that snow is heavy. It can weigh anywhere from 7 pounds (3.2 kg) per cubic foot (0.03 cubic m) to 20 pounds (9.1 kg) per cubic foot. Heavy snow can make roofs cave in, branches break, and power lines fall.

SNOWY SPOTS

If you live in Florida, you probably don't have to worry about blizzards. But if your home is in North Dakota, you should be prepared. Some places are much more likely to get big snowstorms than others. In the United States, they are most common in the Great Plains and Upper Midwest, but blizzards can (and do) happen in other areas.

Conditions must be right for snow and wind. Areas with flat land and few trees do not have protection against very strong, cold winds from farther north. This is the case in parts of Minnesota and the Dakotas. The area gets so many severe storms that it is known as Blizzard Alley.

This map shows the average number of blizzards in the United States from 1959 to 2014. The northern part of the central United States had the greatest number.

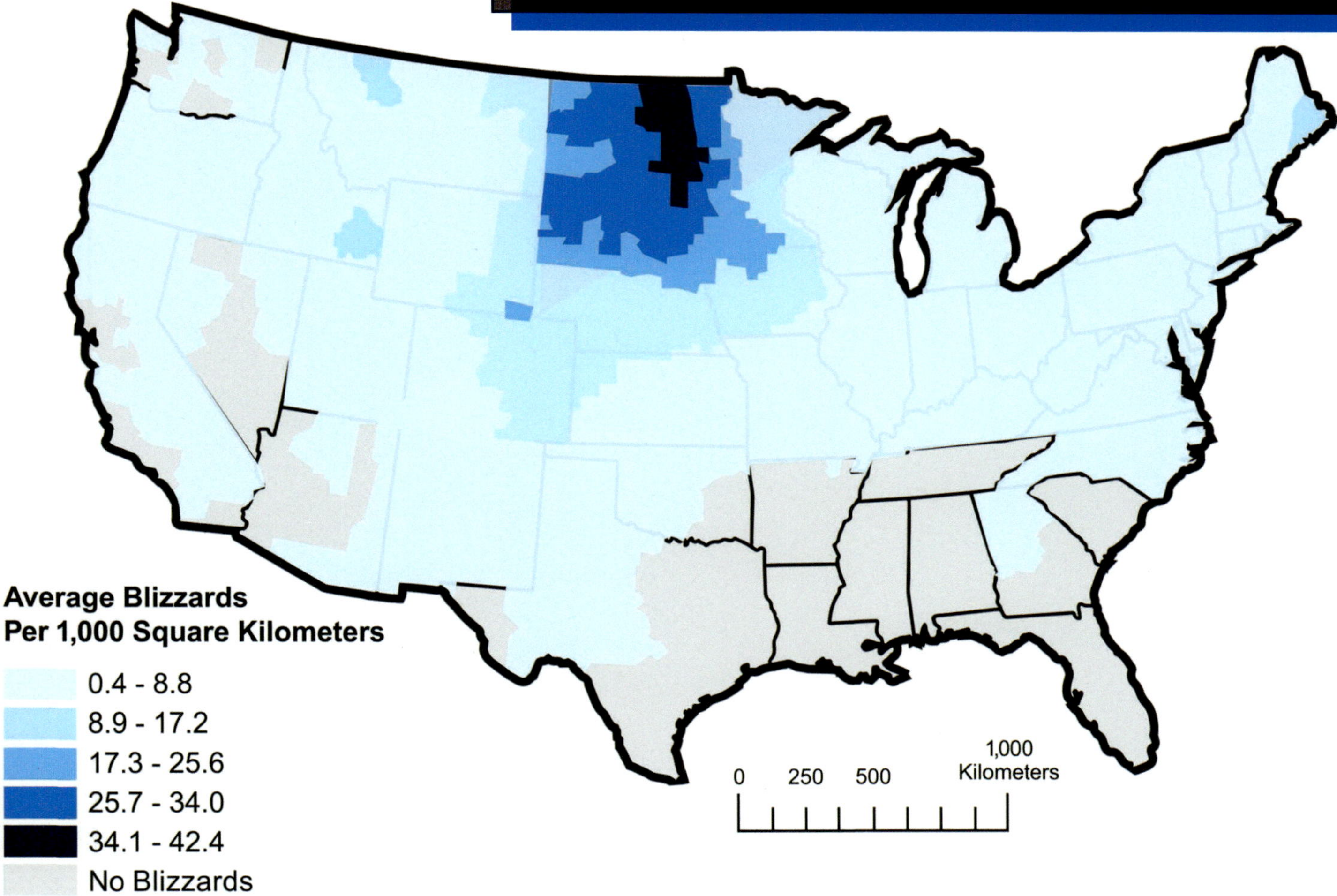

Blame the Arctic

Most areas in the world that have lots of blizzards are in the north. Russia, northeastern Asia, northern Europe, Canada, and the northern United States top the list for most blizzards. All of these regions are areas that are close to the Arctic Circle. Cold winds from the Arctic move south and bump into warmer air. This is how many storms, including blizzards, form.

STORMS TO REMEMBER

There have been many huge, deadly blizzards in the history of the United States. Some of these happened long ago. Scientists did not have the tools to warn people about dangerous weather.

The Great Blizzard of 1888: The deadliest winter storm in American history hit Connecticut, Massachusetts, New Jersey, New York, and Rhode Island. It killed more than 400 people and dropped 40 to 50 inches (101.6 to 127 cm) of snow. The snow buried houses and trains, and high winds sank 200 ships.

The Great Appalachian Storm: In November 1950, a major blizzard moved through the eastern United States. The storm lasted a week, and snow totals reached over 57 inches (144.8 cm). More than 350 people died.

Workers remove snow from New York City streets after the Great Blizzard of 1888.

The Children's Blizzard

January 12, 1888, started out as a nice day in the Northwest Plains. But then temperatures quickly dropped, and winds picked up. People were not prepared for a blizzard. Sadly, many children were sent home from school and died in the sudden storm. In all, 235 people were killed.

A lot of big blizzards happened not too long ago.

- **Snowmageddon:** In February 2010, a giant storm moved from the western United States and Mexico all the way to the East Coast. Areas like Washington, DC; Baltimore, Maryland; and Philadelphia, Pennsylvania, received 20 to 30 inches (50.8 to 76.2 cm) of snow. The blizzard caused more than 40 deaths.

- **The Great Buffalo Blizzard of 2014:** Buffalo, New York, is used to lots of snow. But the blizzard that hit in November 2014 was big even for that area. The storm dumped more than 6 feet (1.8 m) of snow over two days. Many roads were closed, and people were stuck in their cars. In all, 14 people died because of the storm.

Snow Makers

The 2014 blizzard in Buffalo was super-snowy! This was because of lake-effect snow. This happens when cold air moves over the warmer waters of a lake. The chilly air picks up warm water vapor, which rises, cools, and forms narrow bands of clouds. These clouds can make 2 to 3 inches (5 to 7.6 cm) of snow per hour — or more.

This photo shows the approaching wall of snow in Buffalo in November 2014.

GETTING WARMER

Many scientists believe extreme weather is tied to climate change. But Earth's climate has been changing for billions of years. Sometimes it gets colder, and sometimes it gets warmer. Why is climate change a big deal now? It's partly because humans are speeding it up—a lot. Things we do every day are making Earth hotter. This is called global warming.

Some reasons for global warming are out of our control, like changes in the sun. But people play an important part as well. When we drive, cook, or heat our homes, we often use **fossil fuels** like oil and coal. These fuels send gases into the air. The gases trap the sun's heat. Over time, Earth gets warmer.

The Greenhouse Effect

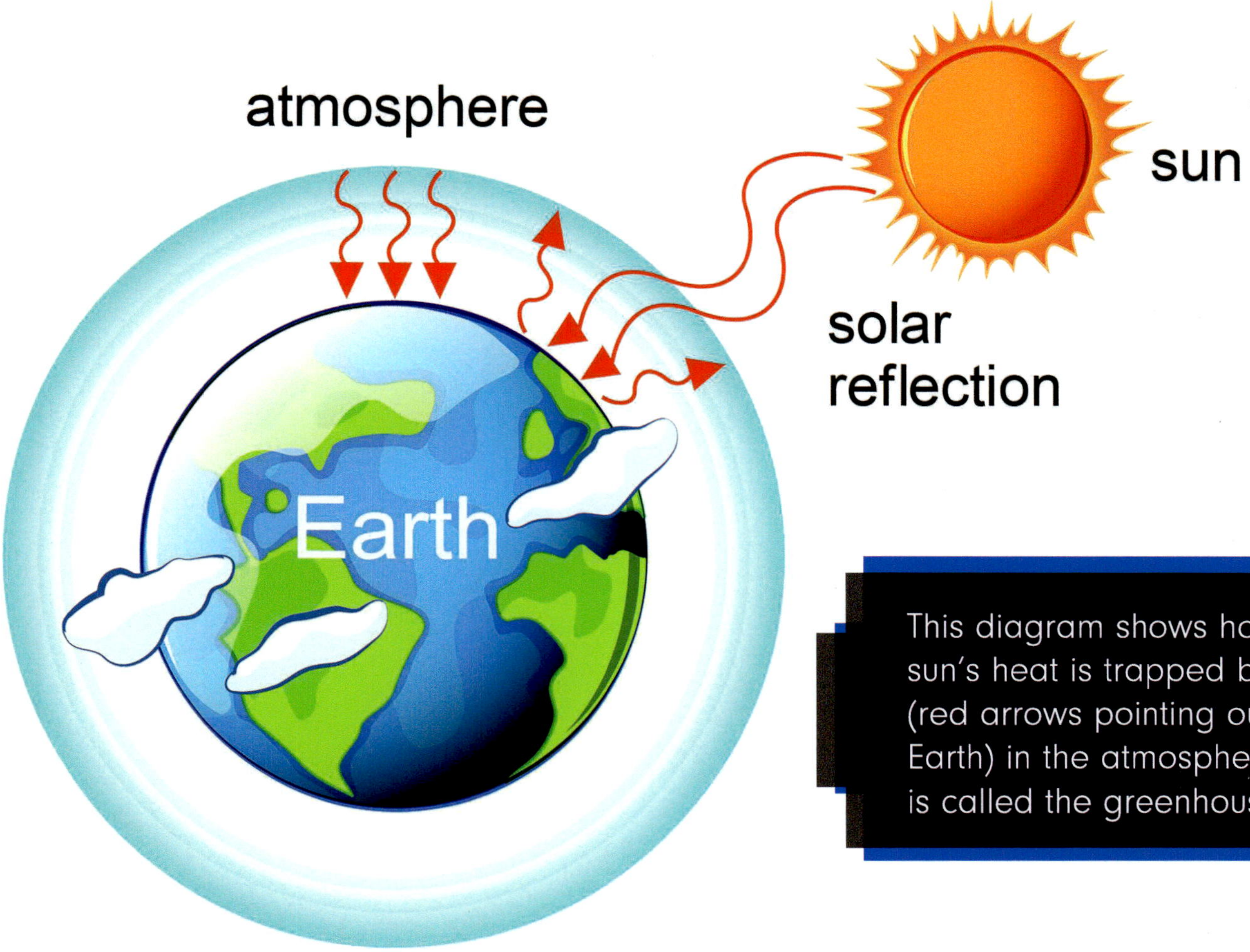

This diagram shows how the sun's heat is trapped by gases (red arrows pointing out from Earth) in the atmosphere. This is called the greenhouse effect.

Melting Away

Global warming causes many changes to our planet. One change is melting snow and ice. Animals such as polar bears and seals are losing their homes. The melting ice also makes the oceans rise. Higher sea levels cause flooding. They also can harm plants and animals that live in or near the water.

GOING TO EXTREMES

If Earth is getting warmer, why would we have more blizzards? Some scientists think that winters in many places will get shorter and have less snow. But they also believe that climate change will cause more extremes in all kinds of weather. This means that there may be fewer storms, but the storms that do happen will be bigger. Let's look at why.

Remember what you learned about the water cycle (page 6). The warmer the oceans get, the more water vapor ends up in the air. This moisture becomes rain or snow. Warmer water also releases more energy into the air. Moisture and energy in the air mean big storms!

This satellite picture shows a blizzard over North America as it appears from space.

More Than Bad Weather

The effects of climate change go far beyond strong storms. As temperatures keep rising, many scientists believe that we will see more wildfires and more **droughts**. As we keep using fossil fuels, harmful gases end up in the ocean and make the water less safe. In turn, this will affect our food supply.

DOING YOUR PART

Climate change and global warming are not going away. But there are simple things you can do to help take care of our planet. Turn off lights when you leave the room. Shut off your computer when you're not using it. Ask your parents to switch your old light bulbs to newer ones that use less energy.

Another great way to help your planet is to spread the word about climate change. Share what you know with your friends. Talk about climate change at school. Young people can be a huge help in slowing down climate change.

Save Our Forests

Trees are very important for a healthy planet. They help remove harmful gases from the atmosphere. But people are cutting down more trees, and forests are disappearing. If you want to help fight climate change, save a tree! Use less paper, recycle, or plant a new tree.

Even young people join protests about climate change.

BIGGER BLIZZARDS?

Blizzards are one of nature's wildest kinds of weather. These cold, windy storms can be scary, dangerous, and even deadly. If you live in a place where a blizzard might happen, plan ahead. Being prepared can help you and your family stay safe.

Big storms are a fact of life. There is a good chance that extreme weather events like blizzards will get worse in years to come. People are responsible for some of the changes that are happening to our planet. But the good news is that it is not too late to make changes for a healthier, safer world. Until then, we could be in for a wild ride!

The Cost of Blizzards

Most severe snowstorms cause a big mess, and cleanup can be very expensive. Lots of equipment is needed to clear roads. A blizzard's high winds and heavy snowfall can damage cars and buildings. A single blizzard can end up costing more than $1 billion to clean up.

Earth is warming up, but severe winter storms such as blizzards may only be getting worse.

GLOSSARY

atmosphere: the mixture of gases that surround a planet

battery: a device that turns chemical energy into electricity

climate change: long-term change in Earth's climate, caused partly by human activities such as burning oil and natural gas

damage: harm

drought: a long period of very dry weather

earthquake: a shaking of the ground caused by the movement of Earth's crust

evaporate: to change from a liquid to a gas

extreme: great or severe

fossil fuel: matter formed over millions of years from plant and animal remains that is burned for power

gust: a sudden, powerful rush of wind

hurricane: a powerful storm that forms over water and causes heavy rainfall and high winds

predict: to guess what will happen in the future based on facts or knowledge

radar: a machine that uses radio waves to locate and identify objects

vapor: a substance that is in the form of a gas or contains very small drops mixed with the air

FOR MORE INFORMATION

BOOKS

Drimmer, Stephanie. *National Geographic Kids Ultimate Weatherpedia.* Washington, DC: National Geographic Kids, 2019.

Tarshis, Lauren. *I Survived the Children's Blizzard, 1888.* New York, NY: Scholastic, 2018.

Zoehfeld, Kathleen Weidner. *What Makes a Blizzard?* New York, NY: HarperCollins, 2018.

WEBSITES

NASA Climate Kids: Weather and Climate
climatekids.nasa.gov/menu/weather-and-climate/
Check out articles, videos, and photos about weather, climate, and our changing planet.

National Geographic Kids: What Is Climate Change?
www.natgeokids.com/uk/discover/geography/general-geography/what-is-climate-change/
Find out all about the causes and effects of climate change and how you can help.

NOAA SciJinks
scijinks.gov/
Learn cool facts about different kinds of weather and get up close with a weather satellite.

INDEX